Still Lo...

Charlie Croker is an author and journalist who for many years now has not gone on holiday without a notebook. His previous books include *The Little Book of Beckham*, *A Game of Three Halves* and *Lost in Translation*. He has also written for *The Times*, the *Independent on Sunday* and the *Spectator*, among others.

'. . . truth is stranger than fiction . . . hilarious . . .'
Sunday Mail

'. . . Croker amusingly highlights the mounting slush
pile of communicative catastrophe . . .'
Scotland on Sunday

'. . . a wonderful collection of recent outrageous
howlers from all over the world.'
Irish Independent

'A perfect book for the loo.'
Sunday Telegraph

Still Lost in Translation

More Misadventures in English Abroad

CHARLIE CROKER

Illustrations by
SANDRA HOWGATE

arrow books

Published by Arrow Books 2008

4 6 8 10 9 7 5

First published in Great Britain in 2007 by
Random House Books
Random House, 20 Vauxhall Bridge Road,
London SW1V 2SA

www.rbooks.co.uk

Addresses for companies within The Random House Group Limited can be found at:
www.randomhouse.co.uk/offices.htm

The Random House Group Limited Reg. No. 954009

A CIP catalogue record for this book
is available from the British Library

ISBN 9780099517566

The Random House Group Limited supports The Forest Stewardship
Council (FSC), the leading international forest certification organisation.
All our titles that are printed on Greenpeace approved FSC certified paper
carry the FSC logo. Our paper procurement policy can be found at:
www.rbooks.co.uk/environment

Typeset by Palimpsest Book Production Limited
Grangemouth, Stirlingshire
Printed in the UK by CPI Bookmarque, Croydon CR0 4TD

Contents

Acknowledgements
vii

Introduction
ix

Trips of the Tongue
1

Inn Trouble
14

Beach Balls Up
46

Snow Joke
50

Sights for Sore Eyes
55

Surprises in Store
67

Taking Care of Business
76

Culture Shocks
80

Making a Meal of It
87

Signs of Madness
98

Health Warnings
113

Style Over Substance
118

Learning the Hard Way
122

Not All Fun and Games
128

The Tangled Web
135

Lost in a Good Book
142

Instruction Ructions
151

Acknowledgements

Many thanks to Nigel, Sophie, Laura, Simon and everyone at Random House for all their help. Thanks also to Sandra Howgate for her wonderful illustrations.

I am indebted, as ever, to Charlie Viney, both for his skills as an agent and his eye for a Swiss menu.

Thanks are due to the following for their alertness in hotels, airports and massage parlours around the world: Rachel Atkins, Kerry Duckworth, Nigel Farndale, Chris Fickling, Joanna Green, Misty Harris, Rob Heeley, Anna Herve, Chris Hope, Pat Lindsay, Chris Pavlo and Matthew Parris. I'm also hugely grateful to the many readers of the first volume who supplied examples for this one.

Finally, thanks to Michael Palin and Paul Bird for kind permission to quote the Japanese fan letter from Michael Palin's 'Diaries 1969–1979, The Python Years' (published by Weidenfeld and Nicolson). The book is a great read, and I heartily recommend you buy it. But only after you've bought this one.

Charlie Croker
July 2007

Introduction

So here we are again, hacking our way through the jungle. Participles dangle to the left of us, erroneous nouns lie to the right, while all around lurk clumps of the densest verbiage known to man. Yes – we're Lost in Translation.

The questions remain. Is an example funnier, for instance, if you can tell what it meant to say (*'Beware of your luggage'*) or if you can't (*'The closed bed points out a time to us which is not so remote'*)? The answer to that one eludes us, but elsewhere truths are starting to emerge. Like the issue of why the Chinese possess quite such a genius for this sort of thing: it's because they're trying so hard with their English in the first place. Anyone who has visited the country will tell you how eager hotel staff, waiters, cabbies and the like are to provide the very warmest of welcomes. Two words are never used when seven will do. In such circumstances you're rarely far from a *'Welcome greet Presence'*.

A similar tendency explains why menus (not just in China but all round the world) prove such fertile territory. Competition between restaurants leads to boasting. A simple description of the food is not enough, so diners find themselves tempted by *'fragrant bone in garlic in strange flavor'*. Or *'three cute prawns suntanning on the rice'*. One restaurant in Cyprus invites you to *'try it and try to forget it'*.

Sometimes the worth of these verbal volleys is more than mere amusement. It's a recognition that other nations have unearthed (albeit accidentally) a linguistic splendour which so-called 'correct' English could never hope to match. Some signs tell you to 'keep off the grass'; a sign in China requests that you *'please treasure the grass'*. And why does the Korean student's farewell card to a teacher – *'I'm sad to separate you'* – pull at the heartstrings so much? Is it because, when it comes to emotion, we mistrust eloquence?

The final point must, of course, be a reminder that as humorous as we find the rest of the world's efforts at English, their skill with our language dwarfs ours with theirs. A touch of humility as we chortle wouldn't go amiss. Nevertheless, chortle we should. It's all you can do when you're Lost in Translation.

*Have you ever found yourself Lost in Translation?
A menu that brought mirth, a sign that made you
snigger, a leaflet that raised a laugh? We'd love to hear
about it for the next volume:*
charlie@lostintranslationbook.com

Trips of the Tongue

They say it's better to travel than to arrive.
Maybe that's something to do with the language you
encounter en route . . .

'Emergency exit' sign at Beijing airport:
Do not use in peacetime.

Sign at Japanese airport:
Departure. Bus stop. Car rectal.

In front of construction works at Bolivian airport:
SORRY FOR THE BOTHER

Jinan International Airport, China:
Careful Landslip, Attention Security.

I

From Orange Airline brochure, Japan:

Orange Airline Incorpolation.

Welcome! Please have a nice trip by airplane.

Our wings provide confidence and comfort all over the world.

We various profit plan is prepared. Please inquire with ease. And we support the comfortable traveling of the skies in customer one by one.

Check-in desk, Ningbo Airport, China:

Please check in animals and alcoholics . . .
Passengers may carry 2 bottle of wine the
volume of 1 or 2 should not be more than
1 kilogram.

On snack handed out on Southern China Airways:

Airline Pulp.

Officialdom gets in on the act too . . .

Mexican immigration form:

Don't forget to sing in the box especified for
the foreigner.

The fields are numbered in order to simplity the
filling out process.

To be fillied out by Tourist . . .

TOURIST . . . WILL NOT BE
AUTHORIZED TO PERFORM LUCRATIVE
OR REMUNERABLE ACTIVITIES.

Brazilian customs form:
4: CURRIED CURRENCY

The fun continues on the ground . . .

On French train:
Do not push yourself out of the window.

Above sink in toilet on train, China:
Don't throw things in the pond.

Sign warning against use of toilet while train is in station, China:
Do not be occupying while stabilizing.

On Chinese train:
In carriage of eating do not sit on floor with legs crossed, as in house. Sit on chair and eat from table. Servant girl bring tea and uneatables.

On-screen instruction, Japanese ticket machine:
Please press the entrained station.

*So much for planes and trains – now for
the automobiles . . .*

Japan:
Caution on passing over pedestrians.

In Japanese car park:
Please get a punch at window No 2.

Sign on windy road in the Himalayas:
Be mild on my curves.

Turkish car hire firm proudly boasts:
Air contagion.

Prague sign:
Non-stop parking.

***

Outside panel beater in Bahrain:
Denting and painting.

***

Small garage in Doha, Qatar:
Punchers repaired here.

***

'Baby on board' sticker, Hong Kong:
Look! Our new baby is on our car!

***

In Japanese car park:
This area is entranse 2nd floor. Don't shit down!!

***

Road signs, China:
To put out Xuanda Expressway.

To put in Jingzhang Expressway.

Rain or snow day. Bridge, slow-driving.

And, warning of descent:
Declimbing path.

Entrance sign at petrol station, Beijing:
Oil gate. / Into.

China:
When you leave car, please turn off door and window, take your valuable object.

Safety instructions for scooter manufactured in Asia:
1. Check the screws, wheels for loosen and abnormality, height of handle and handle before usage.

2. This product is for sliding only, please don't modify this product.

3. For you safety, please put on safety helmet, knee, elbows and wrist guards and put on leisure clothing. Never wear high heel shoes or shoes with slipper sole, avoid headphone and sun glass.

4. Avoid riding together with two persons or on busy street, pedestrian path, gravel road or any place which tend to slippery. We're commend using this product on a parking lot or road without traffic or vacant asphalt game areas.

5. Please don't use by children or person who doesn't read this instruction.

6. Please don't use this product in case of drinking or physically unfit.

7. Please don't use this product in case of raining, snowing, at night.

8. Brake is unable to provide reliable protection on slopes, thus, aware of the speed and make sure you can stop when necessary. But don't reduce the speed too fast, you may fall.

9. Please grip the handles properly while using; besides, don't use this product as a transportation vehicle . . .

10. You may lose your balance while tuming, you are batter to get off or decrease your speed before tuming . . .

. . .

13. This product is suitable for sliding only, do not overestimate your skills. You should adapt the speed to your abiliyt always, it is a good idea to get off if you in doubt of traffic conditions.

14. When self-locking nuts and other self-locking fixings may loose their effectiveness.

When driving yourself can be so dangerous, why not take public transport?

On Prague tram:

Do not expect on floor. Is forbidden to ride on steppes. Do not make speech with man makes tram go. Person without ticket will be persecuted.

Bus stop in Sri Lanka:
MOTOR BUS HALTING PLACE

Sign in window of Japanese ticket office:
You are available at next ticket office.

Sign on the Shanghai metro:
After first under on, do riding with civility.

On bench at a bus stop in Campbell River, British Columbia:
West Coast Prostrate Awareness Society.

Nothing's more fun than messing about on the river. Except, perhaps, messing about with the language . . .

On boat on the Grand Canal, China:
Do not strength your head and hands out of window.

On oil tanker, Alwar, India:
Edible.
Oil Tanker!

Bill of Fayre

Starters

Fish soup with rust and croutons *(France)*

Half a lawyer with prawns *(Switzerland)*

Strong soup with added materials *(Hungary)*

Pee Soup *(Beijing)*

Goulash two cats *(Marianske Lazne, Czech Republic)*

Soup of noodles to the chicken *(La Rochelle)*

Fich-poup *(Majorca)*

Carpaccio of calf burnt to the Savoiarda *(Turin)*

Depressed soup *(Russia)*

Thin of octopus *(Turin)*

Lorry driver soup *(Yaroslav, Russia)*

Mixed Hord Doeuvres *(San Telmo, Majorca)*

Try it and try to forget it *(Cyprus)*

Tourist boat, St Petersburg:

During, at the time of to movements the boat navigation canal to finding on the open deck is forbid!

'Do not disturb' signs on doors of a cruise boat on the Yangtse River, China:

Don't Bother

Notice in bathroom, cruise liner, UK:

To Flush, Push Knob Behind the Seat.

Emergency instructions on a Russian river boat:

In a smoke-filled room, stand as close to the floor as possible . . . When the alarm sounds, return to your cabin and get dressed . . .

Words of wisdom

Beware of your luggage.
(Hotel in Delhi)

Inn Trouble

A good hotel should be a home from home. And if they want to throw in some funny notices around the place, that's a bonus . . .

Hotel in Canary Islands:

Great entertainment – live paella.

❦

Tokyo:

Swindlers dangling around the hotel at night have no connection with the management.

❦

Sweden:

Guests are requested to be as quiet as possible in their rooms after 11pm so as not to disturb the quest in the adjoining room.

On reverse of hotel bill, Portugal:

This establishment is not responsible for money or valuable onjects which have not been left at the desk. It is requested that on leaving, the key be left bell captain's desk.

Small hotel, Cornwall, UK:

Will any guest wishing to take a bath please make arrangements to have one with Mrs Harvey.

Business card for a hotel in Mazar-i-Sharif, Afghanistan:

Tajikistan Hotel – Invited your glads picnics and friendly party.

On the wall of a losman (guest house) in Bali:

You must be welly dressed on the road otherwise you will be arrested and confiscated.

*Hotel, Lake Garda, Italy, offering early
evening aperitifs:*

Martini & nipples.

Brochure for hotel in Yport, France:

This hotel was built for the purpose of the 19ème
siècle to the centre of Yport. Armel et Nadia Lejas
welcome you in an ideal and pleasant framework for
your stay and your meals family . . .

In the section headed . . .

'Activities and leisures to proximity'

you can find . . .

'runs tennis'

and

'aires of games for children'

There is also. . .

'service to two steps of the Casino'

Tourist brochure for the city of Marianske Lazne, Czech Republic, showing which hotels have refrigerators in their room:

Reefer in the room

Budapest hotel with its own dental clinic:

The most modern supplied dental department is available for guests and tourists of the hotel as for the patients coming to a treatment of out-patients . . . At technical manufacturing of crones, bridges and protheses will be used material and technology of firms on world-range.

Dental corrections These corrections occure – at children till the age of 18 without any pain – by the most modern knowledges.

Implantation The dental implantation is a modern process for replacement of missed teeth. The dental implantation solves a lot of problems in connection with the removable protheses. Our dental surgery uses the most modern americal methods.

On website of a hotel in Istanbul:

The hotel was established in 1923 to serve a need of the tourists in the town those days.

The main difference of a wall and a street side room is about the view.

The peaceful secret garden will get you ready for a hurry day ahead not only with the delicious foods served at breakfast, also with the surroundings.

On website of a French hotel:

Nicole and Michel accommodate you in an environment sympathetic nerve and relaxed.

Within a renovated framework, come to release, take glass, to pass one evening between friends, to restore you, make a halt on the road of the holidays, to visit the beautiful area of Burgundy, to finish the evening of "in love" in continuations worthy of your dreams.

Rooms include:

Bathroom where shower with W.C. deprived . . .

9 rooms of 2 people any comfort . . .

2 rooms of 3 people, including 1 with handicapped accesses.

Communicating rooms "Lucienne" with access for
anybody to reduced mobility.

Caption for picture of lounge:
Small show of relaxation.

Caption for picture of seminar room:
Paper-board, markers, sheets, etc, etc to facilitate
work to you and to make one working day one
moment pleasant.

Caption near no picture whatsoever:
the Abuse Alcove is not Dangerous.

The restaurant boasts . . .
a total capacity of 160 forks and spoons, for
your meals of family, of businesses, your
seminars, your meals between friends, at
the head with head . . .

Their specialities include:
The Salmon Smoked House.
The Ham of Stage coach House.
The Sausage of Ass House.
Spotted frog thighs.

The flap with shallot.
The nice one of pig green pepper.

In 'breakfast' section:

The closed bed points out a time to us which is
not so remote

In the 'Evenings of In Love' section:

To reconstitute the history of the impossible lovers
"Tristan & Iseute", come in this world to recognize
themselves, name and lose one in the other, to
disappear and find themselves in another world.
The legend is splendid, because the gesture of
Tristan, moving and terribly human, is nothing
other than the Romance eternal of illegitimate
and impossible passion.

In the 'tourism' section:

Splendid Medieval Village, which has more than one
asset to conquer you

On website of a guest house in Normandy, France:

THE HOUSE
Independent entrance.
At the first floor, a lounge and an adorable
breakfasts room were fitted out for you. During
beautiful days, they can be served to the garden
according to the weather.

ROOMS
In "Agapanthe" in the brown blue and écrues tones,
a bed for 2 persons extra wide (160 by 200) with a
single bed (90 by 180).
You will be seduced by the charm of the bath-room
(with shower) toilet are privative.

THE GARDEN
The garden around the manor house was redrawn
and Marie-Claire, sharing the pleasures of the
gardening with her husband, put all her sensibility
in the service of the nature.
Here and there, benches and deckchairs invite
you to enjoy the peace of the place.
A place where the life is garden and the
painting is garden.

"The first function of a garden it is to look of the happiness and the peace for the spirit"
– Jacques PREVERT

AND NEARBY . . .
In 15 minutes: Rouen La city in hundred bell towers . . .
In 30 minutes: Etretat – Dieppe . . .
At one o'clock: Deauville-Giverny

HOW TO GET THERE:
Highway A 150 then RN 15 . . . Go straight and after the viaduct take to the left way . . . By managing in the village (the church being in your right-hand side) turn to the left way . . .

Swimming pools, it appears, are a particular cause for concern . . .

Notice in Slovenian hotel requests residents not to go through the lobby wearing their . . .
'swimming suite'.

Hotel in Punta Umbria:

The use of the swimming pool is forbidden, while contageous disease is suffered.

The entrance is forbidded in the bathroom area with clothes or street footwear as well as animals.

It is obligatory the use of the walk showers or beacy before the emersion.

It is forbidden to eat up and smoke in the acces and beaches areas.

It is forbidden to give way waste or rubbish in the enclosure, should be used in the waste paper bean or other recipients dedicated to the effect.

It is informed that it exists to the user's disposition a complaints and claims book.

It is forbidden to enter in the swimming pool with animals, instead of that settled down in the law 5/1998, of November 23, relative to the use in Andalusia of dogs guides for people with poor vision.

Cala D'Or:

The swimming pool water is tasted twice a day by the Council.

Greece:

Tonight dinner will be served in the swimming pool

Tenerife:

Balls play is not accepted in the pool area.

Shanghai:

Please not to dive in hotel swim pond. Bottom of pond very hard, and not far from top of water. Please not to crack skull on bottom of pond. If do so, alarm hotel manager at once.

Once you get to your room, though, everything becomes clear. Well, almost . . .

Egypt:

Breakfast is obligatory

Taps in a Beijing hotel room:

No Drinking Without Dealing

A hotel in China, as well as free bath products, offers other items for sale, including boxer shorts labelled . . .

Uncomplimentary Pants

Bill of Fayre

Light Bites

Which on a plate *(Hungary)*

Poked Cutlet Sandwich *(Japan)*

Ham sand witches *(India)*

Very pretty lady salad *(Yaroslav, Russia)*

Fresh stir fried crap with black bean sauce
(Ealing)

Kiss Lorraine *(Kos)*

Homelettes *(Greece)*

Green jewess with jam *(Spain)*

A Confection of Plugs & Geysers *(France)*

Turdey slices *(Tenerife)*

Eggs with Beacons *(Costa Rica)*

Crap meat omelet *(Thailand)*

Sopping kid *(Madeira)*

Restless eggs *('Scrambled eggs' on a 1960s menu
in Mozambique)*

Hen food *(Iran)*

Wood flower picks sea cucumber hoof *(China)*

Big bowl fresh immerse miscellaneous germ *(China)*

Vegetable or meat with spices, rolled in pasty and fried *(London)*

Charcoal Grilled Chicken Wings or fried in garlic source *(London)*

Staft domestos *('stuffed tomatoes' in Skopelos, Greece)*

Deep fried ghost *(China)*

The water boils ridge slice *(China)*

Rice no the shrimp & dipping sauce *(Japan)*

Stewed language in assorted prinkles *(Spain)*

Scaloppa of it gleans to the saffron *(Turin)*

Offering my honored guests delicious meals is my endeavor. Every readiness and efficiency to obtain this target is essential. Kindly assist me in this task by taking at least one meal at my place where my specialty is pig. *(Italy)*

Notice sent to all rooms in Beijing hotel:

The glass exterior window will be cleaned tomorrow. As our Visual Enhancement Team is a bit shy please keep your curtains closed.

Tokyo airport hotel:

Do not open window to prevent a dewdrop or harmful insect entering

Istanbul:

Our room service is 24 hour availabe. Please dial the number "666" for your orders.

Spanish hotel:

The Hotel Hill not be responsible over any object whch hasn't been deposited in the room safety case.

Long trousers/skirts and adequate are compulsory to reach the Dining Room or the Cafeteria.

The guest authorizes, by signing this card, the immediately charge on his Credit Card of any remaining and unpaved debt after his stay.

Budapest:

Forbidden to hang out of hotel window. Person which do so will be charge for clean up mess on footpath.

Instructions for setting wake-up call, Pontarlier, France:

DIAL THE: SIX on your phone and next * with the har atwould you waly like to waked up.

Hotel bathroom, Positano, Italy:

You are Begged to not Throw in the W.C

Absorbent Hygienic And Rolls Of toilet paper kindly

You use the Pouches to Disposition In the special Container.

Thanks! ! ! ! !

Spain:

Service of Laundry: In the locker there is a stock market. It puts the clothes in her and it lowers stock-market to reception. If it gives stock-market in the morning it will receive its clean article in 24H. If the delivery in the evening will receive it to in 36H.

Munich:

In your room you will find a minibar which is filled with alcoholics

Mérida, Mexico:
Segurity Instructive

1. Run by the corridors or by the stairs with humid feet it might cause an accident. We beg yuo to dry your feet before to leave the pool area.

2. In order to avoid accidents getting up or down by the stairs hold your self of the railings.

3. In case of happening any accident into the hotel area get in touch with the telephone operator

or receptionist for medical attention in case of
you to neet it.

4. To use irons or other electric items or to amoke
in the room it might cause damagges on the
fornyture, in those cases the damagges will
be charged on the guests bill.

5. If because to an electronic problem you have to
remain into elevatore wait a couple minutes and
push the reed botton upside of the floors indicatores
bottons. This, it will ring a bell that it'll be attended
by the maintenance personal.

6. The maximum capacity of the elevatore is of
10 persons to excess the weight it might cause that
the elevatore it remains out of order a few hours.

7. The maintenance of the elevatore it's madden
every 15 days and it longs about 30 minutes.

8. If by reansons out of control the hotel would
remain without electricity you have in your room
canddles and matches wich you'll be abble
to use carefully.

9. For a better confort for you and other guests,
please try not to make any mad noices or faights or
close the door strongly.

10. In case of fire in your room or any hotel area, advise immediatly to the operatore or receptionist.

11. For a mayor segurity we have instaled on each corridor an extinguisher wich you'll can to use in case of emergency or advise to the operatore immediatly.

12. Before to check out, we beg you to wait a few minutes after you surrender your room key so the bell boy can check your room in order to be shure that you didn't forget anything in it.

13. Far a mayor confort for you, the hotel has segurity safety box at the front desk, you can leave documents, money or valuables. The receptionist will surrender you a slip for you to request your valuables.

Cologne, Germany:

Repairs: if you have any technical problems in your room in spite of regular controls please fill out the inside paper for repairs and pass it to reception. We are pleased to remove repairs urgently.

Hoi An, Vietnam:
The animal, the weapon, the explosives, inflammable and prostitutes aren't allowed in the hotel.

Leaflet pushed under door of hotel room, China:
Service item

Male sexual funtion
The whole body cares to massage
The foot bottom cares the massage
The thai bealth cares massage
The Russian young lady massage

In the event of a fire it is, of course, vital that you know what to do. Just pray you're not staying in any of these places ...

Krakow, Poland:
Evacuate yourself with the Staircase

Belmar, New Jersey:
In case of fire do not panic and use the fire escape

Hainan Island, China:
Lf you are confound in the room:

1. Do not panic.

2. Wet cloths.

3. Gather enough water to wet cloths.

4. Go at window.

Syria:

In case of fire there is two emergency exit stairs . . .
Upon observing any unordinary aspects (Fire, odour
etc..), please call the operator immediately informing
your room number and your observations.

Please do not loose reason when seeing firemen and
follow their instructions accurately. Disorder and
movement detain are more dangerous than the fire.

Copenhagen:

In fire, the bell rings three times. There is a fine
escape on each floor. For other amusements
see page 3.

Bill of Fayre

Meat dishes

The tripe of water *(China)*

The duck kidney of water *(China)*

Worm pig stomach *(China)*

Bored meat stew *(Slovenia)*

Chicken tikka masala with free rice or nun *(UK)*

Cow's bottom *('rump steak' in Switzerland)*

Bowels stuffed in spleen *(Piraeus)*

Meat in hogs grease *(Pre-war Yugoslavia)*

Cheesebugger and chips *(Greece)*

Chicken, fried come, with rice *(Sumatra)*

Corrugated iron beef *(Beijing)*

Government abuse chicken *(Beijing)*

Saliva Chicken *(Beijing)*

Beef to the cheese *(La Rochelle)*

Skewer of chicken to the bunions *(La Rochelle)*

Bowels with organ Blight *(Greece)*

Thigh with spit *(Greece)*

The believed ham of country *(France)*

Szechwan fragrant celery type fries cow silk
(China)

Melting hazel nuts of pig cheeks the of Var
red wine and spaghettis *(France)*

Oz sirloin on grilled pollen *(Barcelona)*

Roast Mammary Gland of Sheep *(Bulgaria)*

Fine roast pussy or rabbi with stir fry, cook in
wok $2. Passable scrawny chicken with stir fry
$1.50. Bring own chopsticks. *(Hong Kong)*

Slippery meat in king's vegetables in pillar
(China)

The small thigh of lamb roasted with the
furnace *(France)*

Domestic life beef immerses cabbage *(China)*

Lame kebab *(Iran)*

Fuck the salt (beautiful pole) duck chin *(China)*

Instantaneous steak *('minute steak' on a 1960s
menu in Mozambique)*

Carbon burns black bowel *(China)*

Cowboy leg *(China)*

Mixed grill with lamb cubs *(London)*

Loin prick *(Peniche, Portugal)*

Stake Chips *(London)*

Sliced children with broccoli *(China)*

Fuck a bullfrog *(China)*

The rabbit fucks the pot *(China)*

Griled Tornedo with Bearnees Sauce
(Madeira)

Grilled sideburn of pork *(Madeira)*

Fragrant bone in garlic in strange flavor
(China)

Beef of tune to the villainous gravy *(Madeira)*

Litle Pieces of Meat with Fired Chips
(Madeira)

Millefoglie . . . with calf, porky mushrooms . . .
(Turin)

Roastbeef to the fresh grasses *(Turin)*

But be warned – if you eat too much of this,
you risk becoming more fluffy ! *(Poland)*

If hotel life is too daunting, you can always spend the night under canvas . . .

In the toilet block of one French campsite:
To pull, please water the flush

Tank for washing the dishwasher

Notices on various French campsites:

Please do not throw matter in the sink because it constipates the outlets

Any stranger to the camp taken by surprise at the lavaboratories will be subjected to a pain at the discretion of the management.

You are on a tourist site. Please, take care for Rob.

Sometimes the joy of being Lost in Translation can lead to whole new adventures. One English guest at a Prague hotel became fascinated by the establishment's literature . . .

Welcome to our House . . . Let us to offer you some information for your stay:

Reception offered for sale, amongst other items, 'hygienic articles' and 'car security shoes'. . .

and loaned 'irons an iron-tables'

Do you have an interest for a TV-set or a telephone in your room? No problem, ask our reception. These equipments are not included in a basic price for a room, because according to our statistics are many guests, who don't have an interest for it (and that is way we try to spare their money). Rooms for bussines trips have (or don't have) these equipments according to the order of the firm.

Do you have an interest for more towels or for big bath-towels? Do you prefere a change in shorter periods? No problem, ask our reception. (In a case of your extra order, please think also about ecologic problems.)

Should you find our beds too hard, please consider that, according to medical research, they are better for your spine. For example also the owner of this hotel has at home the same beds!

Water from water-network? Water is officially drinkable (but not for sucklings), but we don't recommend to drink it . . . The centre of Prague, where also is our House, has very old water-network (also 120 years!) Water contains lot of iron. That is way hot water can have sometimes a little brown colour. No apprehensions, this is a optical flaw only, not hygienic!

Be careful of your pick pockets especially where is lot of people (metro, tram, shops, in front of historical objects etc).

Prices for taxi are free and can have diverse, we recommend you to ask a taxi-driver for the price before, our reception can inform you about price-estimations (in a case of our taxi company SEDOP we can inform you fix)

<u>Gentlemen, no contacts</u> are recommended <u>with "girls" prostitutes on streets or in bars</u>, mostly they have a connection with gangs (risk of an assault, being drugged with drinks and robbed in a hotel-room. etc). In a case of an interest is better and more safe to visit professional clubs, what are more under a supervision. Some addresses has our reception.

When you pay for an accommodation is our staff obliged to issue and hand over automatically (without being asked by guest) the receipt to you (musters of our receipts you can see on the wall in our reception)

The nearest night medical service . . . the medical service is noticed like 'MC' on the plan of our neighbourhood, what we gave you by check-in

Please to respect kindly the following:

Within our House quite and order are required, especially in rooms in hotel-units and during a night

It is not allowed to move beds and other furniture (a damage is possible)

From the hotel's 'How To Call?' *leaflet:*

The reality, that the telephone apparatus is physicaly in your room, doesn't mean, that it was booked for you a room with a telephone, because our reception schwiches on the telephone line when comes a order.

In our basic prices for an accommodation is namely a using of a telephone in a room not included, because (according to our statistics since 1994) only about 15% of our guests have an interest for a room with a telephone. That is way we can say, that we have another financial politics than other hotels.

. . .

After finishing the telephone call please hang up the apparatus correctly – otherwise your telephone charges will grow up

From the hotel's guest questionnaire:

Could you have a reason for which, due to our fault, you would not like to be accommodated again in our hotel?

From its various confirmation letters:

Re: Accommodation in above noticed period . . . Your reservation we take now like the fix reservation.

Details for the bank transfer see below, please. Fill up carefully all details like is here notice, otherwise the deposit doesn't come or doesn't come in time!

Don't forget, please, about it, otherwise we take this situation, that you don't have more an interest for an accommodation in our hotel.

For a payment of an accommodation we use the same rates (no any commission for us) like banks in the Czech Republic.

We would like to inform you, if you dont come to our hotel on the arrival day (arrival night), that with a sorrow we will have to charge you the first night like the no-arrival fee.

So charmed was the guest, in fact, that he 'misappropriated' a copy of the hotel's leaflet.

Back home, however, guilt got the better of him.
He posted the leaflet back, together with a version in
correct English. The hotel sent him the following reply:

Dear Sir,

a few days before I received your letter. Thank you
very much for the returning of our information
envelopes and especially thank you for the translation
of our information text. This is a grandiose work!
Thank you for your English, thank you for your
time. Now I hope only, that we will have a time to
retype it, because all the time we are in a hurry.

He visited the hotel the following year – the original
leaflet was still in place.

Words of wisdom

You have an unusual equipment for success, use it properly.

(Chinese fortune cookie)

Beach Balls Up

Guide to Buenos Aires:

Several of the local beaches are very copular in the summer.

⚓

Sign on Spanish beach:

Beach of irregular bottoms.

PhiPhi Don, Thailand:

1. Do not catch the small crab along the beach or in the coral

2. Do not take up or damage to coral

3. Do not shoot to bird or catch

4. Do not dig the sand surrounding at the beach

5. Do not throw the trash at the beach or any where

6. Do not loud the sound and disturb to other people

7. Do not fire at the surrounding beach

8. Please help us to clean up with us to every where.

From Headmaster and Comitty of P.P Island Village

At a wadi in Oman:

Drowing accidents are now popular.

Beach bar, Albufeira, Portugal:

It's Not Alowed to Seat in the Chair Without Clothing.

And on the beach itself:

"Smokers?" Use the conical as ashtray and give it back. Keep you beach clean. Users of the granted area.

Ayia Galini Beach, Crete:

Is forbidding the nudism and the camping

Mexico:

Mr. Tourist: The cooperative of production fishery and tourist;
(Pedro el Pescador) autorize for the secretarie of the fishe and tourist in the sonora of state.
To invite with visited and the capture to angostura with end proportional a good service to recover a quota a day for a person to proteccion of the tourist and ourselves.
Recomendate of form your favour cane have and help of proteccion of nets,
with instalation this sing with submerged.
Sicerly the directive.

Words of wisdom

Gusty winds may exist.

(Road sign, New Mexico)

Snow Joke

*Boarding area of gondola in the ski resort of
Les Contamines, near Chamonix, French Alps:*
The doors shut automatically while hooting.

French skiing website's weather report for Valmorel:
Bright and worm day.

Skiing brochure, Heilongjiang province, China:
The time of freeze is long.

Cable car cabin, Huangshan, China:
Smoking, hubbub, spit are forbidden in cabin . . .
The contagious, mental, serious heart patients and
the drunk persons are forbidden to take in the car.

Beidahu Skiing Field cableway station, China:

Points for Attention . . . Refuse the person without ticket or drinking excessively, and the person with hypertension, heart disease, neuropathy and simpleton to get on the lift.

Brochure for ski resort:

Val d'Isere, a resort village, expects you in Winter as well as in Summer for spending relaxing and well-being moments in its comfortable environment.

Words of wisdom

You will gain admiration from your pears.

(Chinese fortune cookie)

Bill of Fayre

Fish dishes

The sand juice are fried the silver snow fish
(China)

Savarin of the sea way chief *(France)*

Gritin of see food *(Agadir, Morocco)*

Chop the strange fish *(Beijing)*

The oil explodes the shrimp *(China)*

Stuffed wolf *('Sea bass' in La Croix Valmer, France)*

Trout of atlas *(Morocco)*

The net of wolf of sea flamed *(France)*

Prawns at "Delicious" *(Madeira)*

Sushi auxiliaries served by pair *(La Rochelle)*

Sad-faced cod *(Russia)*

Paving stone of salomon to the sea of sorrel *(France)*

Grilled 'tigger' king prawns served in a banano leaf *(Spain)*

Fraid squid *(Morocco)*

A quick shave to the iron *('razor shellfish' in Barcelona)*

Homarad "your choise" *(Morocco)*

Burbot shewer *(Morocco)*

Cod net cooked with its skin in Plancha *(France)*

Juice of steams the fish mouth *(China)*

King prawn marinated in mild spies *(London)*

Fuck a fish head *(China)*

We serve dead shrimp on vegetables with a smile. *(China)*

Dumpling stuffed with the ovary and digestive glands of a crab *(China)*

Three cute prawns suntanning on the rice *(China)*

Cod fish at homeway *(Madeira)*

We like 2 please our customers but if u r unhappy please see the manager who will give u total satisfaction. *(Czech republic)*

Sights for Sore Eyes

Sometimes your day really can be a stroll in the park . . .

Sign in Japanese park:
KEEP JAPAN GREEN
DON'T BURN
THE FIRE CHIEF

'Keep off the grass' sign, China:
We can't stand the sight of mattress fragrant grass.

Japan:
The lawn has been preparing. Please, do not enter the lawn.

Sign at the Ethnic Minorities Park, Beijing:
Racist Park.

Park used for dog-walking in the Shunyi district of Beijing:
Dog-Bark Park.

Sign at information centre in Ritan Park, Beijing:
Garden with Curled Poo.

In Japanese national park containing monkeys:
You had better deposit your baggage into the charge free lockers or it will be ours. But we are not interested in your camera. We do not like to be stared at our eyes. If you do so, we are not responsible for what will happen.
We do not hope to be such a monkey.
Please, refrain from
feeding us.

Palaces, monuments, cathedrals – none of them are too grand to bash a little grammar now and then . . .

Sign at the entrance to Korcula Cathedral:
Admitted only decently dressed persons! We beg for silent behaving!

At Hirosaki Castle, Japan:
Smoking should be prohibited inside these facilities.

Please do not graffiti on the wall or anywhere.

Flash photography inside these facilities should be withheld.

Please proceed forward with being directed by museum officials.

Nuisance against the others should be banned in these facilities.

Sign near stone lion, South Korea, warning people not to climb it:
Do not enter.

At tourist attraction, Hainan Island, China:
Please treasure the grass.

China:
Help potect the cultural relecs, help protect
the railings.

'Keep off the grass' sign at Terracotta Warriors Museum, Xi'an:
Cherishing Flowers and Trees.

~~~

On all west exits at subway at Jing An Temple, Shanghai:
Wast Exit.

~~~

In front of a rock garden in the Forbidden City, Beijing:
Please do not climb the rocketry.

~~~

Leaflet from tourist train, Montpellier, France:
In the small street on the right finds him Mikve, bath ritual jewish of the 13es furnished centuries in subsoils of a mansion . . .

To the epoch, she had been built to portion up the old town in the sense North – Southern and to create a rectilinear sylistic avenue hausmanien. it was departing of the garden of the Peyrou and was musting rejoin gardens of the esplanade and puts her of the comedy. Works were not

ever terminated and stopped before the
prefecture . . .

One remarks of share and else of the entry :
"children to lions" . . .

This place is not the uppermost city with 55 ms of
altitude. None real does not pass beyond gardens of
the Peyrou . . .

Aqueduct Clement. This acqueduc, who eats the
water-tower, it is composed of 236 arches . . .
It is surrounded by two staircases shaped like
horseshoe has horse . . .

On your left side, far away, you will be able to
see buttresses Cevennes and celebrates them saint
wolf pick . . .

The universitas médicorum rests in 1220, it
is the elder of Europe and certainly of
the world . . .

Remember of cinema. Facing you, a passing fair
building to rounded form, it would be the place of
cinema hooting with Jacques Brel when this one was
wanting suicide falling by this window . . .

The school of Health creates under convention
joined together then what remains school of Surgery

and so the surgeons found themselves stripped. As well as of other buildings of the city, the hotel became a national good . . .

Main street J Moulin. . . .It is now one of the streets more shopping of Montpellier . . .

Beside the Black Dragon Pool, a lake near Lijang:
Take care! Fall into water carefully!

At base of Japanese volcano:
Now Mt. Aso in strong volcanism and is ejectting sulfurous acid gas but we will warn those who have the asthma. The trouble with the respiratory organs not to go.

Peruvian tourist brochure:
Macchu Picchu is an Inca fortress, considered unparalleled all over the world, due to its completely inexpugnable situation.

Travel agency brochure, Kalimantan, Indonesia:

Far up the river your journey is through mostly primary forest with impenetrable undergrowth, Giant Orchids, Mangrove flowers, huge tress with puthon crapping for branches and tropical bulfrongs.

Publicity material for the Museum of Rasputin in the village of Pokrovskoye:

Since Rasputin – a personality unusual, extraordinary, encircled ensemble of myths and legends, the interest in him was always enormous, moreover regardless of social origins of people – from the worker before the minister.

To Collect material we have begun as far back as 1990, when were live some old-timers sowed Pokrovskogo, remembered Rasputina . . . Certainly, all this was difficult collect, since pass already years . . .

To manage also to gain authentic photographs Grigoria Efimovicha and its family with grant inscriptions, personal notes Rasputina . . . (Part of these documents we for the first time publishes in this book).

Storied group Boney-M, sings in 70-h s its superheat "Rasputin", too has visited Pokrovskoe and sing famous canto in walls our small chamber museum. For sowed this was an event.

In spite of famous guests and enormous pleasure from the contact with the people a work a museum is not revenue. So we have decided heaven and earth, tinned as a fee for this book, start on the building repair-museum.

⋙

Signs at the Golden Summit of the holy mountain Emei Shan, Sichuan:

Taking Cable car, you can pass through heavy clouds and mists, enjoy a wonderful bird's eye view, feel wafting like god and fascinated by the volling billous of cloud, practices height of galleys, sheer cliff, sky-high galley. The cable car is safety and linance, comfortable and saving time . . .

Stand on the tops the beautiful landscaps and the elegent mountains show in your eyes.here you can also see the sunrise and the sunset, the birds flying on the sky. Walking slowly on the forest, the green fir around you, the wind touch your face, all of this let you torget the unhappy.

At Summer Palace, Beijing:

No depicting !

Sign at Sigri, Lesbos, denoting the 'petrified forest':

TOWARDS TEMPORARY PETRIFIED MUSEUM

Museum, Prague:

Please your luggage give to the wardrobe.

Cathedral, Cancun, Mexico:

Please keep loud, wild babes out of the sanctuary.

'Restricted access' sign, Yonghe Temple, Beijing:

The visitor halts.

Hamarikyu Garden, Tokyo:

CAUTION, admission ticket of Hamarikyu-garden cannot do refund after having had you buy it.

⏤⏤

Sign at ruins, Beijing:

To protect cultural relic no carving. In order to keep fit no spitting.

⏤⏤

For sheer effort, you'd struggle to beat the Ming Tombs in Beijing . . .

CHERISH THE CULTURAL RELIC PLEASE DON'T SCRIBBLE.

The Back Side Hall in the Palace.

Environmental sanitation of the scenic spot requires your conserve.

. . . but the Great Wall of China manages it . . .

No smerking.

No fire in the fire forbidden area.

Please buy your ticket consciously.

Words of wisdom

Jerusalem – there's no such city!

(Tourism brochure trying to say 'Jerusalem – there's no city like it!')

Surprises in Store

*A healthy dose of retail therapy can do us all good.
Especially when the signs are so entertaining . . .*

El Corte Inglés department store, Marbella, Spain:
Do not let clothes into the changing rooms.

*Notice behind the customer service desk of a grocery
store, Portimao, Portugal:*
Selling of alcoholic drink is forbidden to minors
of 16 years old and to those who are notoriously
drunk or to the ones who appear to have psychic
abnormities.

In various Japanese shops:
Any assistance? We can help you with our pleasure.

Beware of people

Please don't carry into a store such as a drink.

CAUTION. This cashier can't exchange for money.
If you need it. Please go to the service counter.

A shoplifter is a crime. I notify the police, when
it is found.

To buy it even by one person for a lot of customers,
our shop makes it assume one person sales in a part
of commodity. Please refrain from re-purchase after
accounting. Moreover, please acknowledge that
sales to the resale purpose and this trader make it
refuse beforehand.

To the visitor of accounts.
CAUTION !!
Counterfeit currency and forgery card incidents are
occurring frequently.
Since there is a case where I am allowed to check a
bill, by way of precaution in the case of accounts,
please forgive.

I need your help well cooperation with an under-
standing of a visitor.

VIP REST ROOM. At our shop, the exclusive medal is distributed to the visitor by whom use is done in a charged toilet for nothing. Please offer the staff of a store before use.

Please do not try any earrings on for the sanitation.

We do not take the bill which will start by the account number CB of series in U.S. dollar 100$ in 2001. This series is because imitation is circulating in large quantities in the world recently.

Sign in Chinese shop:
My balls are sold downstairs

Over a jewelry store in Taiwan:
Glod and Silver

Camera shop outside the Forbidden City, Beijing:
DIGITAL PICTURE FAST FLUSHING

Bill of Fayre

Vegetarian selection

Vegetarian stew with cow *(Yaroslav, Russia)*

Pocked-face Ladies Tofu *(Beijing)*

Fork Stew *(Rome)*

Maize mousse on small mushrooms salad and
cereal bread crunchy *(Barcelona)*

Thousand sheet of mozzarella and tomatos to
the caviar of aubergines and parmesan, basil
(France)

Benumbed hot vegetables fries fuck silk
(China)

Vegetables coated with butter served with
deeps *(London)*

Get on the wild plants *(Japan)*

Get on a raw egg *(Japan)*

Spaghetti to the guitar *(Turin)*

Happy Your Pocket ! *(Japan)*

Sign near garden centre, Suffolk, UK:
Parking for plants

Former name of Al Risala Bakery in Masalla, Bahrain:
The Massage Bakery (Al Risala actually translates as 'The Message')

Name of Japanese men's clothes store:
Nudy Boy

Name of fabric embroidery business, Bangkok:
Porn Tip

***

Sign in Beijing store:
To sell inside the commodity space all acceping money sipe supplys examineing the price service.

***

In window of a shop advertising a sale, Hong Kong:
More less!

***

Over the door of a tailor's shop in Sharjah, displaying a large gilt button:
The Golden Bottom

***

Signs at ZaZa City shopping mall, Hamamatsu, Japan:
It is the 10:00 opening.
However, this entrance opens by a delay for several minutes since 10:00. Excuse me, but hurried one please use an entrances expect this entrance.

By laws and ordinances, it is all the buildings prohibition of smoking. What can smoke become only a place of chart below. Please refrain from the use of a minor.

Reverse direction run prohibition of an escalator. There is a danger that I am hurt. I do not bear responsibility of an injury by this.

Please be careful so that child is not idle with an escalator. I do fall and might be hurt when I play here. When I saw a person doing a dangerous act, please call out to the person.

Toledo, Spain:
Frozen ice available here.

Inscription on zip-up shopping bag, Tokyo:
This your useful friend, having simple and fashionable exciting, will be active in your life.

Of course nowadays you don't even need to leave home to go shopping . . .

eBay listing from Germany:

Offer only even if you it to really buy liked

▰▰▰

eBay advert:

The trousers preventing water for baby

You are bidding on Brand new diaper. Layer adopt dry clean net surface, have scattered heat, let in air waiting for effect, protect baby young tender skin very goodly. Middle-level waterproof cloth go through shrink draw material processing handling, pulling force is strong, completely prevent leakage, beautiful again durable. The most outer use fine 100% cotton material and relevant assist material seam system, make baby comfortable. Trousers pipe adept high-grade material, from flexible elasticity material seam system, take action freely, use is convenient.

Words of wisdom

Don't forget you are always on our minds.

(Chinese fortune cookie)

Taking Care of Business

If you want to succeed in business you've really got to sell yourself. Some people manage it better than others . . .

Catalogue promoting various Czech environmental technology companies:

At the own projecting of water supplies buildings, it is self-evident to use the means of modern computing technique.

One company's product was . . .

checked at state institute and can use mark of the highest quality. We are awaiting for you at our firm.

Advert in Bombay (which doesn't actually mention what the product is):

I request with folded hands, kindly once visit and justify my items and rates.

Programme distributed at party, Japan:

Wish! The end time of a meeting or when it gets drunk most, I will take photograph one by one. Please give me cooperation. Although it is slight time, please spend pleasant time today so that one time which cannot be forgotton comes.

Flyer distributed by Polish cleaner soliciting work in Watford:

I have one year of experience in England.
I have the references.
If you are interesting call me please.

Japanese business report:

Hiher price range have decreased little by little in JAPAN. But number of customer can't spread sudden change. So in order to keeping proceed, raising unit price of this range is very important theme.

Job advert, Japan Times, *stating that applicants of either gender are welcome:*

No limit on sex.

Response to travel expenses claim, UK:

Your application is refused on the grounds that I suspect you are using your car as a convenience.

Words of wisdom

People and flowers, plants help each other in breath, if you pick the flowers they will die, and you will reduce your life too.

(At the Simatai section of the Great Wall of China)

Culture Shocks

Why not enjoy a visit to the theatre or cinema? You might get more than you bargained for . . .

Russian woman asking male British companion if he would like to remove his coat as they enter a theatre:

Would you like to undress?

From the ATT Tokyo Guide, an English magazine distributed free at hotels:

Kabukiza Theater. The theatre which excellent lines exist, and is famous. Be brilliant, and the stage equipped with is proud of Kabukiza.

Tokyo International Forum. Various events are done. As a foothold of active international interchange, a multiporpose can utilize it. The open space that imaged one garden between a hall building and glass buildings is space of spacious rest.

Ueno Zoo. The zoo which was made for the first time in Japan. Show an animal equal to or more than 361 kinds including a giant panda of popularity.

Tokyo IMAX Theater. Can enjoy the picture which puts on exclusive glasses, and is full of a sense of reality. 9/2, 2000-3/2, 2001, It has 'Michale Joedan to the MAX' for foreign his fan it is perfect English version!

Mecca of sumo, Ryogoku. If Akihabara is Mecca of an electricity product, the two countries is Mecca of sumo. Several times sumo tournaments are done in a year. A beer hall and a sumo wrestler are daily, and an appetite famous sumo wrestler's meal shop to grind scatters at the outskirts of Ryogoku station a lot.

On door of theatre dressing room, China:
Rest and tiring room for impersonators.

Taiwanese subtitling, in the Uma Thurman film
My Super Ex-Girlfriend, *of 'We have a zero-tolerance policy for sexual harassment':*
We hold the highest standards for sexual harassment.

1950s cinema hoarding in Lugano, advertising The
Flame and the Flesh:
The Light and the Meat.

Or perhaps music's more your thing . . .

Sign, Cyprus:
Life music.

Song title on pirated Pink Floyd CD, Hong Kong:
Come Fartably Numb.

Leaflet with CD of youth choir, Ekaterinburg, Russia:
What the reason for the unique feature of the Choirs?
The managers of 'Aurora' apply the advanced
methods of children's vocal development combining
them with the rich experience as Choirs Masters.
It allows then to bring up practically all children
without any screening thanks to identification and
development of there musical capabilities, careful

formation of vocal voice and thanks to faith in
every child talent . . .

Being taught to modern vocal technology children
become possessors of white spirit vocal diapason
that allow them to perform different musical works
of masterly composers of Renaissance to works
of modern out choirs that our rich in most
difficult vocal tricks . . .

Constant intercourse with the master pieces of
Choir music make the children's private world moke
rich, make them inspired and help to form there
personality . . .

Then again, there's always home entertainment . . .

On sports DVDs, Beijing:

. . . His dreamy family attracts the whole global
eyes. He is David Beckham.

. . . He faces the AIDS with smile. He is Magic
Johnson.

Translation, in 1977 Japanese fan letter to Michael Palin, of the Monty Python sketch title 'Upper Class Twit of the Year':

The Aristocratic Deciding Foolish No. 1 Guy

From Japanese computer games:

Blast Off: To push start only 1 player button, Go next and Entry your name

Pro Wrestling: A winner is you!

Captain America And The Avengers: Why should it goes well?

Persona 2: Let's Positive Thinking!

Subtitles from martial art movies, Hong Kong:

Your spear is useless . . . You better use it for mixing excretory.

Now I feel flatulent, and you did it.

My innards have all been disturbed by him.

That may disarray my intestines.

I please your uterus. You kiss my toes. It's fair.

This is the Martial Arts Competition, not a place for fighting!

Words of wisdom

Keep fire in safe hands, we live in a safe world.

(China)

Making a Meal of It

*Feeling peckish? You soon will be, after these
mouth-watering descriptions . . .*

On chocolate snack, China:
This tastiness cannot be carried, even with both
hands.

Japanese breakfast pastry:
Through years of experience, Doutor Danish is
produced from the finest materials to create a happy
time on tables.

On packet of 'Saying Plum Candies', China:
Hey, So delicious, Let us try it fast.

Packaging on 'Nguan Heng Chan' tea:

SPECIAL HERBING TEA
Suitable for all ages to reduce weight with efficiency and safe.

Suitable for all diet person who can't reduce weight by any method, have no any exercises and can't control eating.

PREPARATION
Just drop – tea in a glass of hot water for 20–30 minutes, drink every night before bed. You'll see the result in 1–2 weeks.

SPECIAL QUALIFICATION
This tea is really best for the person with fatty belly there is no laxative affect.

On Japanese bread packaging:
Take me home, let's make happy in your basket!

Packet of instant noodles, China:
Convenient noodles

Tea cookies, Japan:
This is natural deliciousness given from warm solar light and a rich field. Attach it to time of your wonderful tea. Please ear it on the tea time of afternoon.

✦✦✦

Japanese rice tea cakes:
Burning politely, one by one, these cakes send deliciousness to you.

✦✦✦

Japanese chocolate:
Taste with which the softness of a raw chocolate and the softness of rich cake are mixed and fascinated is the highest wonderful confectionery.

✦✦✦

On cake packaging, Japan:
We baked it assorting our various deliciousness with our whole heart. We bring you the deliciousness which spread fully in your mouth.

Cheese cake, Japan:

Tokyo Cheese Cake. Enjoy the sweetness and natural flavor. This is an elegant, European-style cake including enough cheese made getting a favour of nature in plenty. Please try one at your happy tea time.

On Japanese drinks vending machine:

SOFT DRINKS – Fresh drinking makes your special breaktime much comfortable.
COFFEE – You are served good taste, when you enjoy rest.

Poster advertising chain of cafés, Japan:

Café Miami
Since 1943

We established a fine coffee. What everybody can say TASTY! It's fresh, so mild, with some special coffee's bitter and sour taste. LET'S HAVE SUCH A COFFEE! NOW!

On drinks vending machine, Hamamatsu, Japan:

When you have felt thirst in your heart, you are in need of an oasis for quench your thirst. Your heart are thirsting for a good feeling of place.

On side of bread company's van, Hamamatsu, Japan:

Uncle quattro wants that you are pleased. So that each of bread is baking fresh-baked and put him heart into it. Everytime, everyplace waiting for you!!

Dydo coffee, Japan:

There's a gallon of deliciousness in every drop.

Japanese orange juice:

Just like feeling a fruit in just season itself.

On pack of sandwiches, Crete:

Best before seven days later

Japanese advert:

Why does coffee taste SO good when you're naked with your family?!

What's in a name? Sometimes, you hope, not very much . . .

Brand of Spanish coffee:
Hooker

Japanese biscuit:
Crack Sandwich

Belgian beer:
Pshit (the P is silent)

Spanish sliced bread:
Bimbo

Chinese snack:
Burned Meat Biscuits

Of course you can't beat home cooking ...

Instructions to guests in a Mallorcan country house:
Please wimp the pan with oil before use so that we can all enjoy a happy future with our frying pan

Bill of Fayre

Side Orders

Sweat & Sour Sauce *(Tashkent)*

Crap in the Grass *(Beijing)*

Out of work to the map *(La Rochelle)*

Holy stone *(La Rochelle)*

Assortment of sofas of rice *(La Rochelle)*

Smashed pots *(Greece)*

Peppertree stuff *(Greece)*

Potato diped in better *(London)*

Monkey dung *(Russia)*

Rurality salad *(China)*

Fresh vegetables . . . sprinkled with almond
and sultan's *(London)*

Fried dope *(Marianske Lazne, Czech Republic)*

Spanish and seasonal potato wages *(London)*

We might serve you breakfast here.
(Chiang Mai)

Recipe supplied with a paella pan:

Instructions to cook one "Paella"

The following articles are required:

Olive oil: 45 grames by person
Rice 100 grames by person
Flesh meat Of chicken, rabbit, duck, pig, etc., what
one wishes. Instead of flesh meat, it may be also
cooked with shell-fish.
Peas, artichokes, green beans, according to consumer
taste. With someone of these culinary vegetables
only, it may be cooked.

Water It must reach a level up of one centimeter of
the frying-pan border with the supject, it be not
poured out to boil.

COOKING PROCESS

The flesh meat will be cut in pieces of an
approximate egg's size.

Olive oils is put into the frying-pan in the
aforementioned quantity and when it is very warm,
the flesh meat is thrown, being fried slightly until it
shows a gilt colour. Small pieces of ripe tomato and
one little spoon of grinded large pepper will be
added, and all this be turned upside down into the

frying-pan. At once, it is added the desired culinary vegetables and the water. Salt at will.

The fire is vivified until the culinary vegetables and the flesh meat may be well cooked, without it leaves one moment to boil.

Once all well cooked, the rice is added in the quantity mentioned, procuring it be well distributed throughout the frying-pan. The fire is vivified again until the rice be half cooked. Since this moment, the fire is gradually taken away to leave it at a half ebullition until it be cooked. When the frying-pan is put away from the fire, it is leaved some minutes to rest before serving at the table.

Words of wisdom

Residents refuse to be placed in chutes.

(Tower block in Birmingham)

Signs of Madness

It's a confusing world out there. Just as well the signs make everything so clear . . .

Lesbos:

Do not get in. There are wild cows

Spanish building site:

Not an entrance to no workers.

Port of Jeddah:

You are required to declare all sorts of private things.

In an Italian McDonald's, warning of a wet floor, and attempting to say 'Caution':

Refund !

Various Japanese signs:
No smorking.

Notice of take staircase:

Fasten armrest by order, please don't ambulate in staircase.
Children and old folks take staircase ought to accompany by keeper.
Please don't resort and diaport at passageway.
Strictly prohibit bestride the armrest.
Bicycle don't take the staircase.

Don't protrude the tartness and keenness out the staircase.

Crime prevention camera is during an operation. Pay attention to hand baggage sufficiently.

Please take yourself to anything you like

Above Japanese door handle:

Auto Rock

By Japanese lift:

There is a possibility that a hand and a leg is pinched by the elevator.

Hostess bar, Kakegawa:

Sorry, we decline foreigners to enter.

By escalator, Hamamatsu:

This escalator can stop suddenly. Please use an elevator.

Outside Japanese apartment building:

It is directions garbage other than this building, and forbids!! A fine is obtained when illegal abandonment is carried out!!

Banner in Japan after World War II, when General Douglas MacArthur was being touted in America as a presidential candidate:

WE PRAY FOR MACARTHUR'S ERECTION

Various Chinese signs:

Smoking is prohibited if you will be fined 50 yuan.

If in trouble find police.

Don't forget to take your thing.

No striding.

UNCLEAR POWER PLANT.

By push-button light switch, Italy:
Light Puss Here

⬤⬤⬤

'No entry' sign:
Danger! Inhibition astraddle transgress.

⬤⬤⬤

'Emergency Exit' sign:
Extraordinary Door.

⬤⬤⬤

*On litter bins, encouraging individual responsibility
for the environment:*
Protect CircumStance begin with me.

⬤⬤⬤

Sign for a hand dryer:
Bake the Cell Phone.

⬤⬤⬤

Exhibition hall, Shanghai:
Many Function Hall.

Various Beijing signs:

Forbidden: Prostitution, gambling and drag abuse!

Speaking cellphone strictly prohibited when thunderstorm.

Being urgent call 110 quickly.

Sign on escalator in the city's Xidan district:

The too longer, too higher, overweight and the dangerous things are not allowed to be carried. The older, the children, the deformities, the patients and the pregnant women should take the escalator with his guardian together.

'No shouting' sign:

No noising.

Name of apartment building:

An Australian Lady and Her Lifestyle.

Lefkas, Greece:

MINISTRY OF CULTURE NO TRANSPASSING VIOLATORS WILL BE PERSECUTED

Sign displayed by street fortune teller in Chinatown, NYC:

Help you look your fortune. Hundred per cent true. i am speak English. Trust me 35 years job.

Restaurant in ski resort of Saalbach, Austria:

No toilet using allowed without a konsummation.

In window of Chinese restaurant, Tallahassee, Florida:

NO SUNDAY

Near the security entrance to a bank on the Costa Blanca:

ATTENTION! FOR NORMS OF SECURITY THE ACCESS TO THE OFFICE FOR THE SLUICE. THANK YOU.

Japanese café:

Please Keep chair on position and Keep table cleaned after dying. Thanks for you corporation.

On the Avenue of Stars, Kowloon, Hong Kong:

Care the lovely plants.

Outside a mosque, Istanbul:

Before entering this mosque.
Please remove your shoes.
Please remove your socks.
Please remove your hat.
Thank you for your co-ordination.

Portovenere, Italy:

GROTTA BYRON

THIS GROTTO
WAS THE INSPIRATION OF
LORD BYRON
IT RECORDS THE IMMORTAL POET
WHO

Near building works in Hong Kong apartment block:

We are sorry any unconvenience caused.

Madeira:

Improper water for human consumption

Estate agent listing, Exeter:

A unique feature of this superbly equipped kitchen
must surely be the inclusion of an inbuilt deep friar.

Pub, Ratho, near Edinburgh:

Baby & Toddler Hanging Room

Can you smell smoke . . . ?

'In case of a forest fire . . .' sign, holiday home,
southern France:

Fire instruction:
It's imperatif to follow the safety instruction . . .
Close you the gas bottles, those for itself outside the
house may be . . .
At first water you the external walls and wood parts
of the house, then bring you the hose into safety
(you will need him after the conflagration).
Do you supply themselves with flashlights as the
electric current can be disturbed . . .
If you have a producing or timber house, you look
up a neighbor with a massif house . . .
If smoke should penetrate into the rooms, you
preserve rest and place pieces of cloth in front of
the door chinks.
Do never leave the house in the moment if the
conflagration sweeps over its house.

Fire hose in the Trust Mart, MingHang, Shanghai:
Fire Cock.

Zhouzhuang, China:

Potential danger is worse than naked fire. Precaution before salvation. Fire can be devastating.

The smallest room can have the biggest signs. And you thought it was just a case of remembering to wash your hands . . .

Japan:

For Restrooms, Go back toward your behind.

Women's toilet, Japan:

You lady will push this button before leaving.

Above entrance to men's toilet, Japan:

May I ask forguest Please reftain no check good.

Plastic signs (available for purchase) indicating male and female toilets, Japan:

Lavatory. It has separated to the male and the woman. Don't mistake.

Japan:

For keeping the toilet clean and tidy, please dump at the dustbin.

Anacapri, Italy:

Panties hygenic of emergency euros 2.50.

Notice in a sandwich shop in Plaza de Independencia, Gerona, Spain, telling guests that toilets are kept locked:

Ask for the key to the staff

Men's toilet, China, next to illustration of foot pressing pedal:

Please press hard on cock for water.

A public house in Dungeness, Kent:

GENTLEMEN / TOILETS

Sorry for the condition of our toilets this is due to a car accident.

Shanghai:
Please would paper chuck in wastebin
Thank you!

Men's toilet, Oriental Pearl Tower, Shanghai:
Do not throw urine around.

Disabled toilet signs, China:
Deformed man toilet

and

Crippled restroom.

*Of course if you don't like the signs, you can always
make your own . . .*

Graffiti, Malmo:
Together we're too many!

Graffiti, Bromley-by-Bow Tube station, London:
SAP – Save Are Planet

Words of wisdom

Question Authority.
(Sign for help desk at a Chinese train station)

Health Warnings

We all like to stay in the best of health. Whether we understand how we've managed it is a different matter . . .

Notice at public spa in Karlovy Vary, Czech Republic

1) For the assurance of the undisturbed course of the drinking cure and the hygienical protection of the objects engaged for the serving of mineral waters in the colonnades and at the places connecting with the colonnades there is forbidden;

entrance in dirty or otherwise unsuitable dress awaking public nuisance . . .

throwing away of wastes out of detertmined litters and all other pollution . . .

using of the water from the spring's vases to different purposes than drinking . . .

carrying on of the sale, public street production

(musical, concert, theatre activities, variety and artistic production, production of people's amusement,) painting of pictures or carrying on of all earning activities without permission . . .

2) In the spaces of the colonnades there is forbidden the entrance with the baby-carriages at the time of the drinking cure.

On packaging of Chinese health product:

We distil botanical elite to produce this product by scientific craft. It is maked for anthropometrics by physiological capability and biodegradable intimat interplay, it has a bactericidal and antiphlogistic role. It also can remedy masculine impotence or caduceus flower of coition. The woman of erotic apthy is remedied to be classy.

USAGE: Jet this matter around pubes then the magical impression will appear amid five or ten minutes.

Health and safety document, UK:
Vegetarian food must be kept separate from meat
and clearly ladelled.

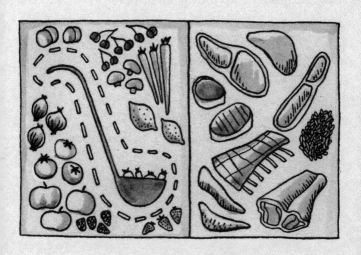

Notice on a door in Sana'a, Yemen:
PHYSIO THE RAPIST

Sign in hospital, Wuhan, China:
Prevent Health Care Section.

On Chinese electric pain-relief device:
Broad and Profound Chinese Traditional Medicine
Deducts Infinite Technological Apotheosis!

Sign outside cottage hospital, Caribbean:
Dont park here, hearse calls daily.

At Northampton General Hospital:
Family Planning Advice: Use rear entrance.

Words of wisdom

Because of your melodic nature, the moonlight
never misses an appointment.

(Chinese fortune cookie)

Style Over Substance

Keeping healthy is important – but so is keeping up appearances . . .

Hairdressing salon in Ghent, Belgium:
Brushing of Watergolf

Japanese barber:
Heads Cutting Y1500. For Bald Men Y900.

On bottle of Japanese nail polish remover:
Nail remover

On Japanese box of tissues:
Skin will be touched softly and gently by 100% high quality pulp.

On Japanese beauty product:

Marine collagen from the mysterious bounties of the sea. Further beauty will be advanced with the supple skin.

On Japanese bath foam:

The fragrance has been closed to us as one of fashion. And now, it is loved as essence that makes feeling relax in the daily life. The perfume bath is a series of popular fragrance. You can expect mental health and beauty from wonderful bath life, because floral and fruity fragrance will remain for you after bathing. Please enjoy bath time!

Label on pair of jeans bought in Greece:

FINE GOODS
WE MAKE NEW
QUALITY FEANE
FOR ALL MODERN
PROFFESSION
AND OFFERING
BASIC GOOD
LOOKING

EVER STINGLY
AUTHENTIC JEANS
GET IMPORTANS
HENPOSITION FIT
AUTHENTIC LOOK
TAPER FROM
HIGH TO ANKLE
HAVE FUN

On T-shirt, Miyajima:

You are the only one
catching eyes on court
Promises you
Chris Evert

Washing instructions with an item of clothing, UK:
PLEASE WASH ON THE OTHER SIDE.

Words of wisdom

If you're happy and you know it, and you realy
want to show it, if you're happy and you know it,
eat a monkey.

(Chinese fortune cookie)

Learning the Hard Way

A good education is vital if you want to get on in the world. There might be a few stumbles along the way, though . . .

Dictation from a university student, Isfahan, Iran:

My penis blue.

Introduction to an essay entitled 'The Night Before Ramadan' by a trainee nurse, Bahrain:

What I like most the night before Ramadan is a really large male.

Description of an electrical experiment by a trainee technician in Bahrain:

When the current flew, the light glew.

From various Korean students:

Translation of the story of Abraham:

His speech was prediction . . . They had been walked
without power, at least they arrived that God
ordered him that place. Abraham made an alter that
place and spreaded wood . . . When he know his
death that was God's meaning, He gave to God his
body with happy . . . And God watched his faithful
servant Abraham that he really do too sacrifice with
his discontent with his endless love behind Abraham
. . . Suddenly, They had been heard on urgently
great voice from the pick. That sounds like that God
was anxious. "Abraham, Abraham, . . . You don't
touch your son to your arm. You don't anything." . . .
They had been took each other and no speech too
happy. It had been too glorious . . . At that time,
Abraham has been saw a ram that its horn was
caught to forest.

Advice on passing one's driving test:

Do you want a driver's license? If you do, DON'T
GIVE UP. Succeed is close of us always. Look at

me. I am full of confidence. The only rest thing is to buy a car.

Essay:

MAKING A LOVE

I'd like to making a love in my life. Because of, Life and love are made for future but these not Racing. The Racing makes only competive. So, I think that the making is creative action.

I have some principle that the making a love need to everyone. Because, The making need to someone's help. If we could helping each other, Happy life would opening to us.

I have a girl-friend who is nurse and twenty-five years old. Therefor, we have a promise to marriage on next year. I'd like to making a love with her not Racing.

On child's notebook, Japan:

The Bunnies are very gluttonous. Why don't we put our favorite flags on the omelets? Good Tasty!

On student's notebook:

My heart is very flammable when I see your beautiful eyes.

Messages on students' farewell card to their English teacher:

You have a beautiful mind. I saw it.

I'm sad to separate you.

You was a good teacher.

I feel cold when I see you.

Russian teacher shouting at noisy class:
With you I feel myself in kindergarten!

Question on exam paper, eastern India:
When a mountain forming granite, lava is what?

Sign at Chinese university:
The following behaviors are perhibited in Pastrol
Education Area:

Do not be naked and other unbehaviors.
Do not litter the trash around.
Cars and bikes are not allowed to enter this area
without permission.
Do not bring dangerous stuff.
Do not follow the instruction on using these facility.

*Sign at the University of Nottingham, Ningbo, China
(the country's first foreign-run university):*
Warm Suggestion: Please keep your
valuables properly!

Words of wisdom

Confucius say you have heart as big as Texas.

(Chinese fortune cookie)

Not All Fun and Games

Perhaps you like some activity in your downtime . . .

Sign at inflatable slide, Jeddah, Saudi Arabia:

Thereto each participant taken circumspection and the carefulness the aquitable.

Thereto each participant dependents the instructions of the operator and the administration not quaered from regulation infracting.

▰▰▰

Brochure for theme park, Japan:

The story of each riding is different. Many people cannot help riding again and again.

▰▰▰

Chinese paragliding site:

Site of jumping umbrella

Bill of Fayre

Desserts

Pleasant aftertaste *(China)*

Trinned peaches *(Majorca)*

Pyjama swelt *(Majorca)*

Rape, sailor style *(Spain)*

Creeps Suzette *(Madeira)*

Tarts for your election *(Spain)*

Chocolate mousse house *(France)*

Custard the caramel house *(France)*

The tart at the whisky *(Menorca)*

Ice Cream with Rubber Chocolate *(Bulgaria)*

Turkish Sweat of the Day *(Erzerum)*

Drinks

Coke (COCA COCA) *(China)*

Flesh Juice *(Japan)*

Alcools *(Japan)*

You may find our wine prices exuberant. *(Warsaw)*

He/she came in a bottle *('wine by the bottle' in Aguas Calientes, Spain)*

Cup of chino *(Beachport, South Australia)*

Small two pots of heads *(Oriental Plaza, Beijing)*

Christmas Bland *(Coffee available at Starbucks, Beijing)*

Our café – a sweat place to eat! *(Turkey)*

Then again, there's always the sporting life . . .

Online contact form of a Spanish golf hotel:

If he wants Enlarged Information on anyone of the services of those that prepares our company . . ., stuff the form that appears next, and in a brief space of time, we will contact you. Remember that he also has the possibility to contact with us through the addresses and telephones that you appear to I tweeted of page.

The hotel's golf rules include:

2. FILIBUSTER: a) MOVABLE: the stones in the bunkers . . . b) INAMOVIBLES: – The trees of the field marked with white painting. – The hoses of WATERING FOR LEAK.

3. ELECTRIC CABLES. If a ball hits any electric line that crosses the field, the blow it will be annulled and she will repeat the blow without penalty.

4. LAND IN REPAIR. The areas of the field marked with stakes blue and white lines . . . Please, REPAIR THE CHOPS, COVER THE you ITCH IN THE GREENS AND PLANE THE FOOTFALLS IN THE BUNKERS. LEAVE

STEP TO THE GRUPOS MAS RÁPIDOS.
THE NONFULFILMENT OF THESE
NORMS will BE PENALIZABLE FOR THE
COMMITTEE.

More from the hotel's website:

In our Social Club he will be able to enjoy the
cafeteria services, bar and restaurant, in those which
prove at any hour of the day an exquisite kitchen to
the purest mediterranean style, dishes of the earth
able to capture the most demanding diner.

We also have a wide space with pools; infantile park
with nursery for the smallest, multy-sport and other
facilities for the practice of the tennis, the paddle
and the horsy one.

A without end of services to be able to enjoy a
wonderful stay. Wardrobes, clever and to point to be
used in any moment of the game day for the
indefatigable professional sportsmen and amateur
that enjoy this sport.

. . .

Furthermore, Spain a modem country . . . has turned
into one of the most competitive countries regarding
the touristic arca.

*Malaysian subtitling, in a television programme, of
'she died in a freak rugby accident':*

She died in a rugby match for people with
deformities

Slogan at a sporting event in pre-democracy Hungary:

Sports in the rotting capitalist countries are the
declared enemy of the Socialist Athletes who
consider it their duty to worth the superiority of
the Socialist races.

Female Norwegian football player:

I tried to screw the ball in the goal

Words of wisdom

Bring your wife to look like the camel.
(Egypt)

The Tangled Web

*We live in an age of instant communication. Perhaps
sometimes that isn't such a good thing . . .*

E-mail from Italian person apologising for being late:
I do hope we did not cause you any incontinence.

*E-mail from the ticket office of the French
Tennis Federation:*
We are pleased to inform that your order has
been confirmated.

Spam e-mail:
Greetings Increase your volume in just days Take
this and your woman will be speechless Surely you
only dream of it But some of us think it's
impossible Have you ever wished to have more
intense final?

E-mail from patisserie, Limassol, Cyprus:

The creative team of Fleurie Patisserie in Limassol has out a new goal as well: to make up this Easter festivities more glamorous for all of us! As base always the Belgian chocolate Callebaut plus a touch of finesse, art and fantasy . . .

An erotic game of the chocolate that flirts with the dry fruits, the nuts and the silver pearls who at the end becomes a much closed friend with the artistic boxes & ribbons! They are available in unique designs and limited shapes!

We deliver in all cities, all our products! And all these, just because style & finesse can not be hidden!!

E-mail from French woman to her English cousin, asking advice on a forthcoming visit to London:

We'd like to visit some great shop (Harrold's . . .) and, if it's possible for us, to visit a television's building our participate in the audience at an television or radio's emission.

After the visit, she reports a safe journey back, but adds:

I have been an achehead because I too overdued
to gin.

Of course the internet is about more than just e-mail . . .

Advert placed by woman on internet dating site, USA:

Hello hello hello. I am young and noninhibited. I
look sort of like the devil. Blonde and luxurious,
with thighs look like toothpick.

My interests include motorcycle. Are you the right man for me?

Do you enjoy dressing up in police costume? Are you close to my age and live nearby? Do you LOVE to get messages on your back and shoulder after a hard day at work? Please write back to me. My ideal date is somewhere long ago. Castles! and princesses!!!! If you want a real princess, send me an email!

If you send me a picture of your penis then I will erase right nowand vomit. No please!!!!! Also, if you cannt rate yourself at least 85/100 in terms of how you rate yourself, don't answer.

I am looking for education and jokes.
TALL not fat. Not skinny ears.

This is Ulysses S Grant. Please love greal heros of this great country, and of my country too!

Noodles!!

Cardboard sign outside webcafé, Japan:
Welcome to you use Internet. You can use Internet here. If you use internet, please come in.

Sign advertising internet banking at hotel's own bank, Hotel Rossiya, Moscow:
Bank's services for natural and artificial persons

Computers can improve your life . . .

On a German software package:
– The on-measure solution for everybody
– We do not let our potential customers
roam in the fog
– Correct against the customer, friendly in the team
– Safe and powerful solution for the cashless
payment in restaurants and coffee shops of company
gastronomy and through sales automates and in
shops of company sales
– In order to create the necessary premises we are
entering your questions, ideas, desires and ameliora-
tion propositions into our new customer database

. . . but they can also ruin it . . .

Error message, Japan:

MS Word can't open the file . . . probably he is damaged !

Words of wisdom

What you left behind is more mellow than wine.

(Chinese fortune cookie)

Lost in a Good Book

*An ancient Arabic saying claims that a book is like a
garden you keep in your pocket. It looks like these
could do with a bit of weeding . . .*

*Excerpts from book about the legends of Santiago de
Compostella, translated by the Spaniard Alfredo Padilla:*

Introduction:

We were trying to account the most important the
Santiago's Road legends. Our purpose is that you
know this ones, with on easy and funny way. In
heather case this book means separates the history
and the legends, so the magic is insight of the free
interpretation of our readers.

From The Fight between Roldan and
the Giant Ferragut
After a long fight, the combat doesn't decide in

favor of none of both and already entrance the night, in an act of nobility, they decide a truce for to rest and to continue up-to-date following.

From Roldan

They were these crossing the narrow pass of Roncevalles, when they are attacked by an army of more than a hundred thousand men that little by little goes them annihilating. Nothing they wasn't could make, except fought until the end. When the emperor came with his army, Only that he found it was bodies deads.

From The Bewitched Place of Irati

This queen, died poisoned and during her life she acted in an evil way against the Catholics to those that she destroyed her churches and her houses. After dying, their body was stolen for you licked them of dragon body and woman's head and the storm nights she destroyed the churches that there were for the surroundings.

And finally, from The Robbery of The Bells

Some type of divine punishment receives

Almanzor, because your horse dies exploded after drinking water of a fountain.

In 1855 Pedro Carolino published The New Guide of the Conversation in Portuguese and English. *This was ambitious, as he didn't actually speak the second of those languages. Instead he wrote his guide using a Portuguese-French phrase book and a French-English dictionary:*

Dedication: 'We expect then, who the little book (for the care what we wrote him, and for her typographical correction) that may be worth the acceptation of the studious persons, and especially of the Youth, at which we dedicate him particularly.'

In the 'Familiar Phrases' Section:
Dry this wine.
He has tost his all good.
Dress my horse.
A throat's ill.

Phrases for a Portuguese visitor to use in England:
You hear the birds gurgling ?

Since you not go out, I shall go out not I neither.
These apricots and these peaches make me and
to come water in mouth.

'Idiotisms and Proverbs':

Nothing some money, nothing of Swiss.
He sin in trouble water.
After the paunch comes the dance.
The stone as roll not, heap up not foam.
He is beggar as a church rat.
Friendship of a child is water into a basket.

'Fishes' include:

hedge hog, a sorte of fish, wolf, torpedo, snail and
sea-calf.

Other entries include:

To craunch a marmoset.

The walls have hearsay.

He go to four feet.

Is sure the road?

He know ride horse.

What o'clock is it?

That not says a word, consent.

What do him?

I have mind to vomit.

That pond it seems me many multiplied of fishes let
us amuse rather to the fishing.

I know well who I have to make.

Leaflet in Mexican book store:

In the books of Mr Rosas Solaegui you will find the
most rich folklore this region. Happening political,
sociable, artistic, historic. Beside custom and all you
need know Oaxaca. Do you buy city's bookstore
either you ask for at his author.

From Italian guide book to the UK:

London is a poetic, visionary, abstract and metaphysical city finally. Whichever pays the right attention to the study of its map and cartography, even if it is of poor quality, sees a long and thrilling poem in its toponymy and the names of the places are so evocative that they become as heavy as elephants. Its restaurants feature the famous sole fish of Denver and the city, one of push bottoms of World economy.

Title of self-help book by Japanese author Hiroyuki Nishigaki:

How to Good-Bye Depression: If You Constrict Anus 100 Times Everyday. Malarkey? or Effective Way?

From the author's website:

Constricting anus 100 times is effective for sex hormone, anti-aging, good-bye depression, fine life, beauty treatment, intuition, hair loss, conjugal affection, incontience (middle-aged or old woman). On air at 70 radio talk shows. Such an exercise looks as if you had your dirty weak used car (your body, heart) overhauled at the garage. The overhauled and powered-up glistened car can run smoothly on any bad road. Such an exercise is fuuny, but you can begin to live without complaints and don't hold a grudge under any circumstance. How about you now? Are you exhausting irty black gas from your buttocks or knocking like a dirty weak used car now? You can start seeing results only within a few days or a few weeks or a few months if you begin to do such an exercise everyday. Maybe it can cure the incontience of elderly woman in 3 months or a year so that she will never be reborn as a baby. Hmm, hmm,,,,,,,,,,,,,,.No, better try

List of book titles held by Indira Importers, Jakarta, 1979:

The Golden Gate *by Alistair MacLean* – Alistair / Golden Gote

Doctor Zhivago *by Boris Pasternak* – Bories / Doctor Zhivogo

. . . *and elsewhere as* Borris / Doctor Chivago

The Guns of Navarone *by Alistair MacLean* –
Alistair / The Guns at Navorome

. . . and elsewhere as The Guns at Navorene

Force 10 From Navarone *by Alistair MacLean* –
Founce to from Navoreme

Fear Is The Key *by Alistair MacLean* –
Alistair / Flak is the key

The Call Of The Pines *by Lucy Walker* –
Luky / The call the pines

Sinister Twilight *by Noel Barber* –
Noel Borker / Ginisteu twenlight

The Labours Of Hercules *by Agatha Christie* –
Agatha / The labours at hercudes

Send Down A Dove *by Charles MacHardy* –
Charles / Send down a dave

Artists In Crime *by Ngaio Marsh* –
Ngaio / Artists in creme

Puppet On A Chain *by Alistair MacLean* –
Alistair / Puppet on a claim

Beasts In My Belfry *by Gerald Durrell* –
Gerald / Beastein my beefry

Words of wisdom

You're toilets.

(Sign to customers in supermarket, Hereford, UK)

Instruction Ructions

*You're three widgets short, you haven't got the right
sort of screwdriver, and the diagrams look like they
were done by Dali. Then things get worse – you
actually try reading the instructions . . .*

For wardrobe manufactured in Japan:

1. Attach upper pipe to pillar pipe and pull out
pillar pipe until the top of upper pipe is reached
to the ceiling.

2. Tighten the short bolt of pipe support
connector all the way.

3. Turn pole to counter clockwise with holding
rubber foot to have secured strong set up or you can
turn rubber foot to clockwise.

4. Measuring appreciate height to hang clothes and
fasten bracket tightly to poles.

5. Pull out cross bar to appreciate length.

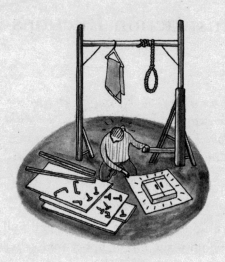

Chinese clockwork radio:

1. Choose the switch (10) the power supply to stir the to close the machine position.

2. Can the turn hour hand or Converse hour hand revolve to shake the generator to turn to move handle to inside to place to refresh the battery to refresh.

3. General circumstance bottom, in a minute of inside continuous 120 turn, and the audibility half an hour is so.

4. Normal circumstance bottom, each one refresh battery can power, turn on electricity 500 times or so. Mightiness suggestion you at Normal circumstance bottom

Italian flat-pack furniture leaflet:
Open the legs and screw as hard as possible.

Attached to a Chinese air compressor:
Attention

1. New air compressors must be poured oil before it starts!!!

2. When using air compressors, and when finding the oil surface go down to the place limited, it must be poured oil in time.

3. Air compressors lacking of oil will cause serious damage.

Written on computer components box in Far East:
Please no plummet

On revolving disco light bought in Thailand:
BRIGHTLY LIGHT – DYNAMIC NO BOUNDS

FADDISH PRESENT – IRIDESCENT GLASSY ORIFICE – CHROMATIC LAMP ROTATION

SUIT BOTH REFINED AND POPULAR TASTES

How to clean the light:
NEUTER SOAP OR CLEANSER AS CLEANING LIQUID IS RECOMMENDABLE

Instructions with loudspeaker system made in China:

Lacking of music, the varied and colorful world will appear pale and weak. MD and MP3 that rise in response to the proper time and conditions are unable to make many friends gathering together to enjoy the romantic music full of dynamic feelings and rich in poetic flavour. The birth of super small Hi-Fi stereo 2.1 active acoustics K8000 brings satisfaction for this pity.

On packaging of guitar holder manufactured in Japan, indicating that it can be used for any type of guitar:
Almighty type.

On the box of a Vietnamese laughing tip-toy:
Can't invert with laugh The laugh begin. you are youthful Automatize. As poke as shaky as shaky as laugh During the use. open the lid of tep and take two cells (NO. 5) in the box. If you want to stop laugh or don't use for a long time. you must take out the cells (This seller have no cells)

Instructions with computer cooling fan, Taiwan:
Going faster is the system job.

On packet of chopsticks, China:
Please to try your Nice Chinese Food With Chopsticks the traditional and typical of Chinese glorious history and cultual.

*On the box of an imitation Winnie-the-Pooh toy
made in China:*

Do you hope to become the friend with me.
Multifunctional intelligent
Fashionably pooh car.
As action it can fluctuate wiggle.
As action, the head can wigwag left and right

Label on electric security gate, Beijing:

The luxuring nothing rail remote controlling
stretches out and draws back the door.

On flower pot, Japan:

The pot, with its rhetroric black & white color,
has been designed to mingle with your most
favorite garden tools with harmony. As you get to
use more, the better it grows on you, and blossoms
your garden life with its old-fashioned simplicity.
Have the most peaceful garden with this lovely
rhetorice pot!!

On Japanese machine used in steel plant:

When service, do not touch it off before ensuring that right/left stays are positioned.

Words of wisdom

Don't behave with cold manners.

(Chinese fortune cookie)

The Importance of Being Trivial

Mark Mason

An entertaining and trivia-filled guide to our obsession with trivia

If you're intrigued by the fact that Jack the Ripper was left-handed, or that Heinz ketchup flows at 0.7 miles per day – and, more importantly, intrigued by why you're intrigued – then this book is required reading. Convinced that our love of trivia must reveal something truly important about us, Mark Mason sets out to discover what that something is. The quest takes him further than he could ever have imagined, from the Natural History Museum to Blackpool Tower, from a pub quiz in Suffolk to the Institute of Cognitive Neuroscience. It leads to lengthy conversations with three professors, the team behind *QI*, and half of Chas and Dave. It even involves a major scientific discovery at the foot of Big Ben.

Mark's journey forces him to re-evaluate everything, from his view of knowledge to his relationship with his girlfriend. Trivia, far from being trivial, leads him to tackle life's fundamental questions. Why is it so difficult to forget that Keith Richards was a choirboy at the Queen's coronation when it's so hard to remember what we did last Thursday? Are men more obsessed with trivia than women? Can it be proved that house flies hum in the key of F? Can anything ever really be proved? And the biggest question of them all: is there a perfect fact, and if so what is it?

arrow books

The Clumsiest People in Europe

Favell Lee Mortimer and Todd Pruzan

Comically insensitive and startlingly opinionated, Mrs Favell Lee Mortimer offers up a hilariously inappropriate account of Victorian prejudices

In the middle of the 1800s, Mrs Favell Lee Mortimer set out to write an ambitious guide to all the nations on Earth. There were just three problems:

- She had never set foot outside Shropshire.
- She was horribly misinformed about virtually every topic she turned her attention to.
- And she was prejudiced against foreigners.

The result was an unintentionally hilarious masterpiece:
'The French like being smart but are not very clean.'
'The Japanese are very polite people – much politer than the Chinese – but very proud.'
'The Scotch will not take much trouble to please strangers.'

In *The Clumsiest People in Europe*, Todd Pruzan has gathered together a selection of Mrs Mortimer's finest moments, celebrating the woman who turned ignorance into an art form.

'Politically incorrect doesn't begin to cover it. Dads of a certain age will adore it.' *Scotland on Sunday*

'. . . extraordinary . . . this book gives a very unusual and rather horrifying insight into the Victorian world view.' *Good Book Guide*

'. . . a real collection of outrageously ill-informed writings. . . you have to admire the nerve of the publishers . . .' *Sunday Telegraph*

'. . . outrageous and gloriously politically incorrect . . .' *Daily Mail*

arrow books

THE POWER OF READING

Visit the Random House website and get connected with information on all our books and authors

EXTRACTS from our recently published books and selected backlist titles

COMPETITIONS AND PRIZE DRAWS Win signed books, audiobooks and more

AUTHOR EVENTS Find out which of our authors are on tour and where you can meet them

LATEST NEWS on bestsellers, awards and new publications

MINISITES with exclusive special features dedicated to our authors and their titles

READING GROUPS Reading guides, special features and all the information you need for your reading group

LISTEN to extracts from the latest audiobook publications

WATCH video clips of interviews and readings with our authors

RANDOM HOUSE INFORMATION including advice for writers, job vacancies and all your general queries answered

Come home to Random House

www.rbooks.co.uk

**Order more Arrow books
from your local bookshop, or have them delivered
direct to your door by Bookpost**

☐ **The Importance of Being Trivial**

Mark Mason   9780099521822   £7.99

☐ **The Clumsiest People in Europe**

Favell Lee Mortimer and
Todd Pruzan   9780099509479   £6.99

Free post and packing
Overseas customers allow £2 per paperback

Phone: 01624 677237

Post: Random House Books
c/o Bookpost, PO Box 29, Douglas, Isle of Man IM99 1BQ

Fax: 01624 670923

email: bookshop@enterprise.net

Cheques (payable to Bookpost) and credit cards accepted

Prices and availability subject to change without notice.
Allow 28 days for delivery.
When placing your order, please state if you do not wish to receive any
additional information.

www.rbooks.co.uk

arrow books